It won't work!

By Janine Amos and Annabel Spenceley
Consultant Rachael Underwood

CHERRYTREE BOOKS

A Cherrytree Book

Designed and produced
by A S Publishing

First published 1999
by Cherrytree Press Ltd
a subsidiary of
The Chivers Company Ltd
Windsor Bridge Road
Bath BA2 3AX

Copyright © Cherrytree Press Ltd 1999

British Library Cataloguing in Publication Data

Amos, Janine
  It won't work!. – (Good friends)
  1.Friendship – Pictorial works – Juvenile literature
  I. Title II.Annabel Spenceley
  302.3'4

ISBN 0 7540 9059 0

Printed in Malaysia

The sandcastle

Jacob is at the seaside with his grandad.
He is building a sandcastle.

Jacob fills his bucket with sand.
He pats it down hard.

He turns the bucket over . . .
and the sand falls out.

"Agh!" screams Jacob.
"It won't work!"

Jacob stamps his feet.
He bursts into tears.

Grandad puts down his paper.
"You sound very angry, Jacob," he says.

Jacob screams even louder.

"I can't do it!" he sobs.
How does Jacob feel?

"You're having a hard time building with this sand," says Grandad.

12

"Yes," agrees Jacob, "it keeps falling out."

"What could you do?" asks Grandad.
Jacob thinks.

He looks at the sand. He looks at the sea.
"I'll make the sand wetter!" says Jacob.

Jacob mixes sea water into the dry sand.

"Will it work now?" he wonders.

"I've done it!" smiles Jacob.
How does Jacob feel now?

The marble game

Alice is playing with her marble game.
She fixes the pieces together.

20

She finishes the last tower.
Now she's ready to send down a marble.

Plop! – the marble drops to the bottom.

"It won't work!" thinks Alice.
How does Alice feel?

24

"What can I do?" she wonders.
She looks hard at the towers.

25

She checks each part.

"Yes!" says Alice, "here's the problem!"

27

She turns the yellow part around.

Alice tests the game again.

This time the marble rolls backwards and forwards all along the run!

31

Sometimes things don't work in the way we want them to. We feel frustrated or angry. It's OK to feel upset when things go wrong.

If something's not working, be a good friend to yourself; take a deep breath and tell yourself that you can do it. Looking at the problem again may help you to solve it. If you feel very upset, talk about it with someone else.